MORE
Welsh Valleys Humour

MORE
Welsh Valleys
Humour

David Jandrell

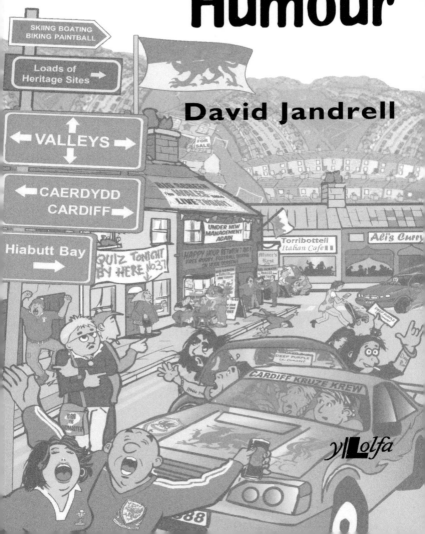

y Lolfa

Illustrations: Siôn Jones
Book design: Y Lolfa

ISBN: 978 - 1 - 8477 - 1952 - 2

Printed on acid-free and partly recycled paper
and published and bound in Wales by
Y Lolfa Cyf., Talybont, Ceredigion SY24 5HE
e-mail ylolfa@ylolfa.com
website www.ylolfa.com
tel. 01970 832 304
fax 01970 832 782

Contents

Introduction

Since *Welsh Valleys Humour* appeared on the shelves in 2004 a lot of people have had an insight into Welsh Valleys life and the humour that goes alongside it. An insight maybe that they would not otherwise have gleaned from the usual sources of regional exposure – media, sitcoms, stereotypes etc.

Having travelled widely in the past, I had become aware that the general concept of the Welsh in parts of the UK that I visited was that we were a race of beer-swilling, rugby-mad sheep farmers, er… and that's it.

I'm not suggesting that the whole of the population of the UK thought that, but I can state categorically here that most of the people that I met were of that opinion.

I remember accompanying some girls to Cardiff on a shopping trip in 1975 during my first term in college and I was shocked by one of the comments made by one of these young ladies – who, by the way, had arrived in Gwent from the heady depths of north Somerset, which is, in reality, not that far away. Her reaction to the Cardiff trip suggested that the distance from her home to Gwent was measured, in her world, in thousands of miles and not in tens of miles which is a more realistic estimate of the space between the two places.

I say this because when we were on the bus coming out of Cardiff, she looked me in the eye and in all seriousness said:

> "Cardiff is great isn't it? Do you know, until I went there today, I always pictured it as a sort of quaint fishing village with a couple of chip shops, ice cream parlours and a few gift shops."

Although this caused a bit of hilarity amongst the other girls who were with us, they also concurred with the original observation that Cardiff was much bigger and 'up to date' than they had imagined. These hailed from Oxfordshire, Hampshire and Cornwall, none of which are noted for being blessed with huge conurbations but still the concept existed that Cardiff and Wales were very 'low profile' in their expectations of what they would find there when they actually visited the place.

I have used this very specific example of *non-Welsh UK-ites'* concept of our land and its inhabitants because I found it to be typical of those who had heard of Wales but never visited – although maybe not as extreme as the Somerset girl's surprise at how advanced we actually were!

So if *Welsh Valleys Humour* has changed just one person's view of us, then it was a success.

Welsh Valleys Humour also opened my eyes to aspects of Welsh life and culture that I didn't address at the time of writing. Since then, many people have approached me with comments like "Why didn't you mention this?", and then described things that they thought would have gone down well if I'd thought about it at the time.

So with these in mind I began to consciously seek out other areas which would have been appropriate to include in the first piece of work – and as a result I noticed a lot more things which may be exclusively Welsh and I have gathered some more endearing foibles for your delectation.

So let's not dawdle about any longer with protracted wordy explanations, eh? Here it is, *More Welsh Valleys Humour*.

DAVID JANDRELL

1. Linguistic Oddities

English in the UK

The language that is predominantly spoken in the UK at the moment is English.

You only have to watch TV to understand that there are countless variations in the way that English is spoken from one place to another.

Soaps are very high profile on TV, and these focus on regional accents and dialects because they are supposed to reflect everyday life and language prevalent in the area where the soap is set. *Coronation Street* deals with everyday life in the north west of England, *Emmerdale* is set in Yorkshire and *Eastenders* reflects Cockney attitudes and language, to name but three.

Whilst there are dramatic variations in pronunciation, grammar and syntax within these different versions of English, they are piped into our front rooms via the TV on a daily basis and, on the whole, we all understand what is going on. We are used to it.

The first time I encountered an accent which was different to my own was when I was a very small child. I cannot remember exactly how old I was but I do know that it happened pre-1960 which would mean that I would have been no older than five. I know it was pre-1960, because it was also pre-*Coronation Street*. If it had been later, I may have seen a few episodes of that Soap and become accustomed to the Lancashire accent and this incident may never have happened.

Want a pwp?

I had gone to call on my friend Steve to go out to play and to look at the pups that their dog Lady had presented them with a few days earlier. It was a Sunday afternoon and Steve's father was having the statutory post-Sunday lunch nap and his mother was washing up in the kitchen. Steve was upstairs pumping up his football.

I sat on the settee and waited for Steve to come downstairs. I could hear the noises of crockery being washed coming from the kitchen and hoped that Steve's father wouldn't wake up and blame me for disturbing his snooze.

Then his mother appeared in the doorway between the living room and the kitchen and asked me if I was OK. I nodded, still not wanting to wake Steve's dad.

She disappeared back into the kitchen and reappeared moments later. This time she was wiping a dinner plate with a teacloth. It was at this point that she uttered those words which will live with me forever. She looked at me and with a huge smile on her face, said:

"Dave, do you want a pup?"

Now I always knew Steve's mum 'talked funny', but I didn't know why.

It wasn't until a few years later that I found out the real reason why – it was because she was from Manchester, and their vowels sound a lot different to the way we say ours.

So, even though Steve's mum was asking me, in good faith, if I wanted a pup, the words that I heard were:

"Dave, do you want a poop?"
(The 'oo' here sounds like the 'oo' in the English 'soot')

Now, in the Valleys, we have a word, 'Pwp' which sounds like 'poop' but it means the same as the English, 'poo'. For a five-year-old Welsh Valleys boy, 'poop' or 'pwp' is 'pwp' and that's that!

My initial reaction was that I couldn't have heard her correctly; I mean Steve's mum didn't actually ask me if I wanted a poo, did she? I just looked down to the floor and shuffled my feet around a bit on their shag pile because I couldn't understand what had just happened. I thought I'd managed to get away with it because she disappeared back into the kitchen. But my fears returned when she re-entered the room, this time with a saucer in her hand. She began to wipe the saucer dry and once again asked:

"Dave, do you want a pup?"

I couldn't stand it any longer! I did hear her correctly: she wants to know if I want a poo. This time I did what any other child in the same position would do – I became hysterical and screamed the place down.

This woke Steve's father and I became even more upset and louder as a result.

Because of the racket I was making, Steve had charged downstairs with the part-inflated football and he, his mum and his father began to quiz me as to why I had suddenly 'gone off on one.'

I was beside myself and couldn't speak – to such an extent that Steve's father put me in his car and took me home.

I couldn't even explain what had happened to my parents – in order to do this I had to use the word 'pwp', which was strictly taboo in those days, especially in front of your parents, and on a Sunday!

My parents thought that they should take me to the doctor to try to get to the bottom of my unexplained crying fit and I managed to calm myself down when I realised that I'd have to say 'pwp' to the doctor as well. Luckily, this 'blew over' very quickly and no mention was made by either my family or Steve's, so the true cause of my outburst was never revealed, until now that is.

Variations in local pronunciation

Listen to a Geordie speaking to a Cornishman and these will be plain to hear. Ask an American, or a German, or a Frenchman to listen to the same conversation and they may doubt that the Geordie and Cornishman were actually speaking the same language as each other.

That aside, I have noticed variations in pronunciation, grammar, syntax within a 10-mile radius of my front door. These are marked differences and I have not noticed them because I have a 'trained ear' for that sort of thing – I have actually misunderstood what people have said to me. In reality, I should not be finding it difficult to communicate with people who reside in areas that are merely five or six stops away on the local bus service. Well, I have!

A good example of this can be illustrated by recounting a conversation between myself and Mike from Abertillery which is a massive 8 miles away from my home. I'd known Mike for a number of years and we'd communicated without any problems until this one time, when he came up to me and said:

"Dai, do you like jars?"

I was hesitant with my reply because I hadn't understood

his question, and when I thought he had waited long enough for a reply I asked:

"What sort of jars do you mean Mike? Jam jars?"
"No, Brecon Jars."

I hadn't realised it but I was being thrown off the scent here by an elongated flattened vowel sound. I'm referring to the vowel sound in Mike's 'jars'. Mike was actually asking me if I liked jazz and was building up to ask me if I wanted to accompany him to the Brecon Jazz Festival.

In a local shop we have two women shop assistants. They work opposite shifts so that when one is working the other is off. One is, like Mike, from Abertillery and the other is local to me.

They each have a very different way of saying "Thank you" when transactions have been completed.

Before I move on, a quick quiz; what do these words have in common?

- Mittens
- Buttons
- Department
- Assortment

In fast speech, people rarely make the 't' sounds in these words. Commonly, the 't' sound is replaced by a throaty pause – a classic example of this would be to imagine a Cockney saying the word 'butter'. Got it? In linguistic terms, this is known as a glottal stop.

Back to the story – when our two ladies say "Thank you" after a sale, a two-syllable phrase, they actually only utter an audible one-syllable sound, which is "Kyou."

They have used a glottal stop to do away with the first part of "Thank", but they retain the 'K' sound and tag the 'you' onto it. The difference between the two shortened words that they use is the way that they pronounce the vowels.

The one who is local to me actually says "Cue", which sounds like the stick you hit the balls with in snooker or maybe a line of people waiting their turn. The lady from Abertillery says, "Cow."

I wonder what the reaction would be if an English person who called into the shop when just passing through would make of the parting comment from whichever of our ladies served them. Can you imagine someone from Surrey leaving the shop after being served by the lady from Abertillery and saying to her husband:

> "I bought a bottle of milk from that woman in the shop and as I was about to leave she called me a cow!!!"

I just had a thought. As these glottal stops usually come in the middle or the end of a word and bearing in mind our shop assistants are beginning their words with one, maybe I have identified a new topic to linguistics – that of the glottal start! Maybe worth thinking about for a second or two? Or perhaps not!

The 'Rogue Yah'

During my working life I had always worked around the Newport area. I then went to work in Ystrad Mynach in 2002, only 7 miles away from my home – but in a different valley! What a difference switching valleys makes.

It was there that I came into contact with people from the Rhymney and Cynon valleys, for the first time! I must admit, it took me until 2008 to fully get used to the language.

On the whole, I must admit I was able to communicate well with all concerned but I did have a few moments of utter confusion. I will illustrate this by telling you the story of the 'mystery Julia' and the strange thing that I call the 'rogue yah'.

I worked for some of the time in an office and occasionally when I picked up an unattended phone that was ringing, there would be someone on the other end asking if they could speak to Julia. As there wasn't a Julia in the office, I would tell the caller that we didn't have anyone by that name in the office and politely end the conversation. This happened maybe half a dozen times over a two-year period and I didn't really think too much about the mystery Julia. I mean, sometimes people ring the wrong number – I thought this was the case here.

In around 2007, I went to a function in the Abercynon area and I became intrigued by one particular woman who was sitting near to us. I was intrigued by her name more than anything else – all the people who spoke to her called her Daphnia.

Now I am perfectly aware of what Daphnia are. I sometimes go out and catch Daphnia, my tropical fish love to eat them. They are small water fleas found in stagnant water.

I must admit, at the start of the night, I wondered why this woman's parents had named her after a water flea, but towards the end of the evening, I spotted her 'table place card' and saw that she had actually been christened Daphne. Suddenly, things started to fit into place.

I had noticed that when we had asked for directions to the venue earlier on in the evening, the person we asked told us that we had to go up the A470, go past Ponty (Pontypridd) and Abercynon would be signposted. What he actually said was:

> "Go up the A470-yah, go past Ponty-yah and you'll start to see signposts for Abercynon."

I realised then for the first time that in this area there was a tendency to add this 'rogue yah' sound to words that ended in an 'e', 'i' or 'y' sound.

In truth I was quite proud of myself; I'd actually 'found out' why Daphne was known locally as Daphnia. As I was wallowing in a great bout of gloating self satisfaction, I was suddenly overcome with a feeling of utter devastation. Utter devastation?

Yes. I don't know what made me think about it at the time, but it came to me in a flash – the true identity of the mystery Julia. It was actually Julie who sat near the phone that I used to pick up when it rang and when she wasn't there.

Somehow I didn't think it was appropriate for me to go into work and say:

> "Oh, by the way Julie, someone rang for you..."

The Statement, Confirm, Question Syndrome

Another thing that caused me confusion in my early days in this new environment was the tendency to add unnecessary phrases into simple sentences. I have called this the 'Make a statement, confirm it and then question what you have just said' syndrome.

Here is an example. I was speaking to a rather large chap from the area and we were swapping information on what we did in our spare time. I told him that I played guitar and he reciprocated with:

> "I play rugby for Bargoed I do, don't I?"

Let's look at this closely. I'll break it down into sections for you. I think there are three well-defined parts to this:

1. I play rugby for Bargoed (here the statement has been made)
2. I do (confirmation of first statement)
3. Don't I? (questioning sections one and two)

When I first heard this my reaction was:

> "Eh? What? Well do you play for Bargoed or not?"
> "Oh aye, I've played for them for about ten years now I have, haven't I."

Here are some more:

> "We went down the club on Friday we did, didn't we?"

> "We haven't known a winter this bad ever we haven't, have we?"

> "Cardiff City just missed out on promotion again they did, didn't they?"

"You wanna keep that dog of yours under control you do, don't you?"

I'm not going to bombard you with any more of these, I'm guessing you get the gist of it by now you do, don't you?

I spoke to Matthew Tucker (with whom I co-wrote *Rubgy Trip Stories*) at length about my bouts of confusion in Ystrad Mynach. As an Ystrad Mynach boy he was able to help me out a lot with my plight and explain a few of the mistakes I'd made.

According to Matthew:

"Well, you are from Newport way. That's England that is. You're all English down there. You can tell by the way you talk. Blinkin' English you are. We're Welsh up here, not like you lot down there, isn't it. Look."

I'm not so sure that I was made to feel better after hearing Matthew's analysis of my problems, but it did confirm that my alleged anglicised roots explained why I had noticed and queried things like 'rogue yahs', glottal stops, glottal starts, make a statement, confirm it and then question what you have just said, syndromes, etc.

At the very least, these observations have given us something to think about anyway.

I'm not suggesting here that I speak properly and that I am taking a large swipe at others and the way they speak – we all have different ways of expressing ourselves and these play a big part in what makes us who we are. Accents allow us to identify with places and groups and we maintain our heritage by the way that we communicate.

Who is right? Who knows? Who's to say? Is there an accent ombudsman? What about Mike's 'Jars' and my 'Jazz', what do you call that type of music?

It's a bit like the English North v. South debate on 'do you say bath or bath?'

To be honest, I'm a neutral. I've always said bath and will continue to do so.

Usser

Here's another very parochial south-east Wales term. I'm not sure how to spell it. I'm not even sure if it's a word in English or Welsh, but it sounds as if it should be Welsh. I have yet to find a Welsh speaker who knows what it is. But ask any non-Welsh speaking south-east Wales dweller what it means and he or she will be able to tell you straightaway.

So what does it mean?

First, let's do a pronunciation exercise. I'll do it in three sections.

> Think of the word 'puss' as in *Puss-in-Boots*.
> Add 'er' – so the word becomes 'pusser'.
> Take the 'p' off, and the word becomes 'usser'.

Got it? Good.

Now an usser is anything that is unspecified whose name is either forgotten or not known. It can be likened to the English thingamajig, whatsitsname, doodah, oojah-kapivvy, thingamabob, etc.

There are a few variants of these English contraptions that are commonly used throughout Wales, these being "wossnim" a version of whatsitsname and "woducall" which is based on "What do you call it", to name but two.

Sometimes my partner and I play a little game in which we try to use all the words in our contraption vocabulary in one conversation – until one of us either blows our top or the initiator of the conversation remembers what the item or person being referred to is called.

For example, my partner may want me to pass the remote control for the TV. In which case she might say:

"Pass the thing."
"Thing?"
"Yeah, you know, the doodah over by there."

Here, I'll look to where she's pointing, pick up an ashtray, wave it at her and say:

"Do you mean the thingamajig?"

"No! The woducall, further over!"

This time I pick up telephone and offer it up.

"You mean the oojah-kapivvy?"
"No! the wossnim, look it's right by the coffee cup!"

Then I pick up the remote control.

"This?"
"Yes."
"You mean the usser, why didn't you say?"
"Just pass it over here."

Sometimes, when neither of us is in a particularly playful mood, these conversations can be very brief, like this recent one:

"Oh, I saw wossnim in the Spar with his missus earlier on."
"Is he alright?"
"Yeah."

"D'ya know what I mean?"

I don't know whether people think I'm a bit thick. I'm beginning to think they do. I don't know why, but nowadays people seem to want to confirm that I've understood what they've just said by tagging on a "D'ya know what I mean?" to the end of every sentence.

"I don't want another drink, I've got work in the morning. D'ya know what I mean?"

"They're a good band, but I wouldn't go to see them live. D'ya know what I mean?"

When I reply, "No, I didn't understand a word of that

mate, can you say it again, only in not such complicated terms," people look at me as if I'm from Mars!

Now if someone said, "The obliquity of the ecliptic is not a fixed quantity but changing over time" in mixed company, I think that a "D'ya know what I mean?" would be an appropriate tag on. This is a complicated sentence.

But there's nothing intrinsically difficult about:

> "I watch *Emmerdale*, but I prefer *Coronation Street*. D'ya know what I mean?"

Do you know what I mean?

Question and answer techniques

Something that I have been aware of for a long time is the tendency for people to not answer a question as it is put. Instead they will give an answer which is an answer to a question which has not been asked – and the response is generally accepted as an appropriate answer. Here is an example.

I was visiting some friends and when I was there some other visitors turned up. We got all the introductions out of the way and we were enjoying a cuppa and chocolate biscuits when one of the other visitors spotted a vase sitting in a display cabinet. She expressed her appreciation for the vase by saying:

"That's a lovely vase, where did you get that from?"

To which the owner replied;

"Oh, I've had it for ages."

Now, the question as to where the vase had been purchased had not been addressed at all. The owner must have obviously thought that the visitor had said, "How long have you had that vase?" because the answer she gave would have been suitable.

Interestingly, the visitor accepted, "Oh, I've had it for ages" as an appropriate response to the question and moved on to another topic.

Here are a few more for your delectation:

"Have you had an invitation to the wedding?"
"It's the same day as the match!"

"Are you enjoying this film?"
"I've seen it before."

"How long are you going to be getting ready?"
"I'm just putting my boots on."

"Do you fancy a cuppa?"
"I haven't sat down all day."

"How often do you bath your dog?"
"Have you ever tried to bath a dog!"

"Did anybody call when I was out?"
"I've been in the shower."

"That's an attractive fish. What type is it?"
"I don't really know where it came from. It kind of 'appeared' in the tank."

"Who do you think will win on Saturday?"
"I'm not interested in rugby."

"What time does the snooker club open?"
"Well, I know it closes at 11pm."

"Is peanut butter good for you or is it fattening?"
"Don't be stupid!"

"Are you in or out tonight?"
"*Midsomer Murders* is on later."

"What do you want for tea tonight?"
"I'm having my hair done straight after work."

I can't quite see the rationale behind these responses. If you look at the questions and the answers given, it seems likely that a large proportion should be "I don't know." There appears to be some sort of reluctance to say "I don't know", so the alternative cryptic answer is given. Here the original questioner has to guess what the answerer thinks from the

WHO DO YOU THINK WILL WIN ON SATURDAY?

I'M GOIN' ON SUNDAY I AM..

THE REF'S FROM DOWN PONTY

THE ART OF CONVERSATIONS ...

answer he/she gives. From my experience, these cryptic answers are very rarely challenged. It's as if the questioner subconsciously thinks "Oo-er... obviously dodgy ground here, I'd better not pursue this. I'll change the subject."

If you do challenge such a response however, you can have a bit of fun – just like the fun I had when I challenged the response to my question, "How far is it from here to Aberdare?"

Here goes:

"How far is it from here to Aberdare?"
"About twenty minutes."
"Since when has distance been measured in minutes?"

"I was merely saying how long it would take me to get there."

"Yeah, but you know where it is, I don't."

"It should still take you about 20 minutes."

"How long it takes surely depends on which way you go and how fast you drive."

"Look, you asked me and I told you, ask someone else if you're not happy."

"Well why don't you just tell me how far it is?"

"I have!"

"No you haven't."

"Oh, I give up!"

The question still stands. How far is it from Ystrad Mynach to Aberdare? Does anybody know?

And talking about things that are 20 minutes away, here is a section on something that's 40 minutes away (from Cwmcarn this time).

2. Changes in the Valley

Since the demise of the pits and the landscaping of the areas that these ugly, filthy places occupied, the topography of the Welsh Valleys has changed considerably. The Valleys have now become very picturesque and attract many more visitors than they had experienced in the past. Historically, Wales had been a holiday favourite for people who headed for the coast, Snowdonia, the Brecon Beacons, etc.

As a child, I remember the village became like a ghost-town during Miners' Fortnight which was usually the last week of July and the first week of August. During this period, the miners vacated the dusty towns and villages and headed for Barry or Porthcawl for a two-week break in the sun.

It was commonplace to refer to Barry and Porthcawl as 'Hiyabutt Bay' in those days; it didn't matter which you were referring to, they both had that pet name.

"Where are you going for your holidays this year?"
"Only Hiyabutt Bay."

The term 'Hiyabutt Bay' came from the continuous airing of "Hiya butt" as miners and their families acknowledged people they knew when walking around the town, the beach, the pub, the caravan site, the funfair, well everywhere really.

It has been reported that 400,000 people arrived in Barry on one day in the 1960s! Can you imagine walking down the promenade on that day?

"Hiya butt." "Hiya butt." "Hiya butt." "Hiya butt." "Hiya butt."
"Hiya butt." "Hiya butt." "Hiya butt." "Hiya butt." "Hiya butt."
"Hiya butt." "Hiya butt." "Hiya butt." "Hiya butt." "Hiya butt."
"Hiya butt." "Hiya butt." "Hiya butt." "Hiya butt." "Hiya butt."
"Hiya butt." "Hiya butt." "Hiya butt." "Hiya butt." "Hiya butt."
"Hiya butt." "Hiya butt." "Hiya butt." "Hiya butt." "Hiya butt."

Enough of that!

I wonder how many people who were present in Barry on that day would believe you if you told them that in the year 2012, there would be massive influxes of tourists heading away from the coast to visit their villages instead. I'm guessing none.

"What the 'ell would anyone want to go there for? There's nothing there, mun!"

Well, that's what people want these days. 'Nothing there' is a big attraction for people, especially when you take into account that the landscape is back as it was before the industrial revolution. The industrial revolution meant that as far as the eye could see the mountains and picturesque Valleys were dominated by huge pit workings and chimneys belching out black smoke 24 hours a day.

Not only has the topography changed, attitudes have also changed a lot, noticeable even in the time since I have graced the planet with my presence!

People have much more leisure time nowadays than when I was a child. There are leisure facilities everywhere – country parks, heritage trails, biking and boating facilities, wildlife sanctuaries, ancient monuments, etc.

on our doorsteps and these are being used by local people on weekends and bank holidays regularly. Of course, the local day trippers mingle with holidaymakers from afar and recommend other centres in the locality – word gets around and soon local treasures become accessible to all.

These cater fully to all visitors, whether local or otherwise by providing eating establishments, toilets, gift shops, visitor centres, information desks, campsites, etc. 'Posh' foreign restaurants have started to spring up in villages attached to these touristy places and people are finding that the grand day out can be finished off perfectly by indulging in an expensive 'slap up' at one of these establishments.

Eating Out

Going out for a meal has grown in popularity since the time when I was a child. We ate at meal times and generally all the food was plain and there was no great fuss made of presentation and the drinking of wine to complement whichever main course you had. You 'ate out' sometimes – if you were shopping you might have dined at the cafeteria in the supermarket you were in, or maybe a chippy, or grabbed a roll and a packet of crisps from a local bakery.

In my late teens, after a night out we would pile into the local chippy or Chinese takeaway after huge drinking bouts – booze always makes you hungry. We always blamed the usual hangover-related headaches and nausea on the meals we'd had, never the booze.

I remember getting home after the chippy and Chinese had shut one night. I had the 'munchies' and decided to make myself a couple of sandwiches. I opened the fridge and spotted a block of cheese the size of a house-brick. Cheese and onion sandwiches immediately sprang to mind. I set about the task and when I'd made my sandwiches, staggered into the front room to eat them and try to catch whatever was left on the TV because, in those days, the three channels we had closed down at about midnight.

My first bite told me that something was wrong. Closer investigation revealed my mistake. I had made myself marzipan and onion sandwiches – not a good mix.

I still maintain though that I'd defy anyone to be able to look at a lump of marzipan in a fridge and be able to tell it's not cheese!

The 'eating out' trend has grown in popularity over the years and nowadays people eat out regularly. So much so that the meal has now become the social occasion. Years ago people ate out as a consequence of being out. Now it has become the reason for going out.

Here is a little story. It is a classic example of the Valley-boy and posh eateries not necessarily being a good mix.

I have not been able to contact the hero of this anecdote to ask his permission to name him here, so for the purpose of relating the story I'll call him Malcolm. I'm sure he won't mind.

Malcolm is a very insular type of chap; doesn't mix well and doesn't travel too far. He lives and works in the village he was born in and hasn't any real reason to leave it. He goes to the local supermarket on a Saturday for the weekly shop and spends a fortnight at the Costa Packet for his summer holidays, and that's that.

There was a rather large 'heavy metal' contingent in his village and when heavy metal gods Deep Purple announced that they were touring, 20 odd years after their last outing, a lot of interest was generated.

They were to do a show in Cardiff and no sooner had the date been announced, a piece of paper appeared on the pub notice board asking people who were interested in going to sign, and if there were enough 'takers' the pub would organise a minibus.

It came as a shock to most when Malcolm's name appeared on the list. Was he actually going to willingly be taken out of the village? Yes – he remembered that back in the 70s he liked Deep Purple and the one LP that he still owned was by the very same outfit.

To most people a trip to see a band was just a case of going and coming back – no big deal really, but for Malcolm there was a lot of planning to do and this involved having knowledge of a full itinerary so that he would be ready for the night.

After liaising with several regular concert goers, he was happy with the itinerary that he was given. This was:

1. Meet in the pub at 6pm
2. Have a few pints
3. Get on the minibus booked for 7pm
4. Have a few cans on the way down to Cardiff
5. Have a few pints in Cardiff on arrival
6. Make their way to the venue for 8.30pm and have a few pints in there
7. Watch the band and have a few pints at the same time
8. Have a few pints after the show
9. Go for a curry and have a few pints in the curry house
10. Get on the minibus to come home – booked for a midnight pick-up

As usual, everything went according to plan until they got to stage 9, the curry. Malcolm had never had a curry in an Indian restaurant before, and had absolutely no idea what any of the items on the menu meant. Luckily enough, for him, the well-seasoned and well-oiled concert goers who had chaperoned Malcolm around for the evening took charge and ordered his meal for him. They did not pull the usual trick of ordering the most viciously hot curry that the house did. They chose a Korma, half and half, Nan and the other usual trimmings for Malcolm to tuck into. Aw, that was nice of them. For the next three months Malcolm talked about nothing else – according to him, not only was it the only night out he'd ever had, it was the best night he'd ever had. He'd seen a live band and had the best meal he'd ever had and it was in a restaurant – he'd never eaten in a restaurant before.

And then life went on as usual… until, about five or six years later, Deep Purple decided to tour again!

Sure enough a piece of paper appeared on the pub notice board seeking interested parties for another trip to see them, and Malcolm's name was the first on the list. He asked for an itinerary, and strangely enough the itinerary was:

1. Meet in the pub at 6pm
2. Have a few pints
3. Get on the minibus booked for 7pm
4. Have a few cans on the way down
5. Have a few pints in Cardiff on arrival
6. Make their way to the venue for 8.30pm and have a few pints in there
7. Watch the band and have a few pints at the same time
8. Have a few pints after the show
9. Go for a curry and have a few pints in the curry house
10. Get on the minibus to come home – booked for a midnight pick-up

Malcolm was about to relive the best night he'd ever had in his life!

As before, all went according to plan and stage 9 did not present a problem for Malcolm, he'd had a curry before hadn't he? He knew exactly what to do. When the waiter asked him what he wanted, Malcolm leaned back in his chair and announced with great authority and confidence:

"I'll have the same as what I had when I was in here the last time, please."

Wow!

Offlese

Not only have eating habits changed, not including Malcolm and to be honest, myself – the whole work ethic seems to be changing to reflect the way that the workforce are adapting to changes in the employment environment following the demise of the pits.

Throughout my career I have noticed a gradual change in the way that people speak to each other in work. We all know that Japanese and Chinese are recognised languages, but over the last decade or so I have recognised another language – one that I will call Offlese. This is the language of the office/workplace.

I first heard it when I joined a new company in the mid-80s. I'd been given the customary tour and been introduced to everyone and had been told what their roles were within the organisation.

When I got back into the office, the big boss arrived, extended his hand and said:

"So, you must be David. Welcome aboard."

I thought, "Welcome aboard? I wasn't aware that I'd just joined the Navy!"

Since then I've taken part in *thought showers* where everyone *touched base* to *make sure we were all singing from the same hymn-sheet* before *shinning up* the proverbial *greasy pole*. You know, *making sure we had all our ducks in a row*.

I thought I'd better become fluent in this language *PDQ* to be honest. I didn't want to make a fool of myself in front of the *fat man in the canoe* did I? This involved two strategies, *blue sky thinking* and the sort that is done *outside the box*. I had to get *up to speed fast* – it was *a big ask* I know, but I was *on the case 24/7.*

Anyway, after I had *drilled down* all the inappropriate non-Offlese terms, I was *going forward* in my quest to avoid being the *Dilbert* in the company.

It nearly went *pear shaped* a few times but I managed to *ramp up at the eleventh hour.*

Even though I had always been taught to avoid clichés like the plague, I had quite a *bumpy ride* and *when all was said and done,* I *up-scaled* by listening to other speakers and I managed to *wash the face* of my problem – it was a sort of *quid pro quo* strategy that *put it to bed* adequately.

When I thought *I had the bandwidth* I decided to *run it by* the *man in the chair* by arranging some *face time* – luckily enough *he had a window* and he was able to see me. He's a bit of a *crackberry* but I decided to *give it my best shot* – I mean, if my arse was on the line, I didn't want any cock-ups. It was a *low hanging fruit scenario* to be honest and now was the time *to run it up the flagpole* and *see who saluted.*

Fortunately the *one-to-one* was a success and I was able to converse with my colleagues in such a way that I was understood and my language didn't become a *negative value driver* to them.

In the end, I became *head honcho* of the *whole shebang* and *wore the crown* until the owners decided to *draw a line under it* and the *whole caboodle* went *down the pan* as a result of *corporate downsizing.*

This is quite a change from the language that I experienced when I checked in on the first day of my working life. This was more like:

> "Alright butt? Ow's it goy-in? See him over by there, he's the bloke ew'll be working with for today. Just take ew round the place a bit first, innit, and he'll show ew the ropes. It's alright working yer, just keep yer 'ead down, arse up and keep yer nose clean and ew'll do alright. Lemme know 'ow you d'get on after before you d'go 'ome."

To be honest, this was the most formal way in which I was spoken to during my time with them. Well, it was my first day! After that, the language was slightly less formal and peppered with expletives, but everyone understood instructions, everyone knew exactly where they stood and everyone got on with each other.

Somehow, I'm not sure that the change has been for the better even if I have managed to get all my ducks in a row... whatever that means.

Yoof culture and language

Over the last few years, I have noticed huge differences in the way that yoof culture has affected language. There seems to be a definite shift towards 'Estuary English' which is why I use the term yoof in favour of youth here. Youths now seem to be referring to themselves as yoofs and talk about 'poplah cultchah' with a clearly detectable London/Cockney sound to it.

Probably one of the most overused 'Welshisms', commonly aired by people who are trying to put on a stereotypical Welsh accent is the inclusion of 'isn't it' at the end of every sentence. Generally, those who try to put on the Welsh accent tag their 'isn't its' onto the most inappropriate opening sentences, like these:

> "I'm off to Cardiff at the weekend, isn't it."
> "If you carry on doing that, I'm going to call the police, isn't it."
> "I'm having a new guitar for Christmas, isn't it."

But nowadays even Welsh kids seem to be phasing out our "isn't it" in favour of the anglicised "innit." Not only is "innit" replacing "isn't it", they are beginning to drop the 't' sound at the end, so what you actually hear is "inni". Another glottal stop!

This adds to the London/Cockney way in which it sounds and it's beginning to become overused. Hardly a sentence goes by without the statutory "innit" finishing it off:

> "Spiderman is a great film, innit."
> "I'm going round my friend's house, innit."
> "Look at my new car, innit."
> "I may have a virus on my computer, innit."

Another strange thing that seems to be gaining in popularity is the addition of unnecessary words into sentences, I guess to stress a point that the speaker is trying to make. So, a person may report to a friend that, "I'm *totally* not going to go out with you, no way innit," or "I'm *absolutely* upgrading my phone at the end of my contract, innit."

Here's another recent development – I hear it a lot these days. I am referring to the throwaway, dismissive and often aggressive 'whatever!' response made to any comment that the recipient is not happy with.

> "I'm sorry to tell you this, but we're going to have to amputate both your legs."
> "Whatever!"

This comment normally follows the adoption of a particular pose – arm outstretched, other hand on hip, a tapping of a foot and eyes raised to the heavens. This normally heralds the end of a conversation because the 'whatever-user' has either been backed into a corner or has been proved wrong and is saying: "You got me there mate, I'm not discussing it any longer. I'm off!"

Verbal communication seems to be moving along in such a way that certain parts are becoming visual. The recipient now seems to have to watch the speaker in order to get the full meaning of the information that is being passed on.

I call it the "Gap after 'like' method".

This transcript of an actual conversation overheard in a queue between two female students at Stand One at Newport bus station and perfectly illustrates this particular trait.

> STUDENT 1: "And he walked in, right, and I was like… (long gap accompanied by a facial gesture and change of posture supposed to convey to the listener what the person was 'like')… and he was like… (another gap, same as above)… and I said to him, I said, 'Oh,' I said, 'It's nice to see you'… (long gap, no facial gestures this time. This secondary gap is designed to create tension)… NOT! And he was like… (gap with a different posture and a different facial expression to depict what 'he' was 'like') … Oh aye, I turned round and told him straight."
>
> STUDENT 2: "You turned round and told him straight, didn't you?"
>
> STUDENT 1: "I sooo told him. Aye, I said it to him, I did."
>
> STUDENT 2: "And what did he say?"
>
> STUDENT 1: "He never said nuffink."

STUDENT 2 "Ah, well that says it all then doesn't it."

STUDENT 1: "It was soooooo not right what he done mind."

STUDENT 2: "Well he shouldn't of should he."

STUDENT 1: "Aye. No! Shouldn't of potched you mean. Specially not with that minger."

STUDENT 2: "Minging is she?"

STUDENT 1: Oh aye, hangin' mun."

STUDENT 2: "What's all that about? Eh?

At this point my bus arrived so I missed the rest of it.

I would like to let you know here, that if you particularly like the 'gap after "like" method' and want to use it for communication purposes, it doesn't work if you are on the phone! I say this because I did observe someone doing this once whilst speaking into a mobile – the only person who was getting the benefit of the raised eyebrows, the pouts and the hand-on-hip gestures, was me!

I can't understand why people keep telling me they'll see me later. It's a popular parting comment these days. I was on my way home the other night and I stopped to exchange pleasantries with a colleague in the car park. His last words to me were, "See you later." He lives 40 miles away from Cwmcarn!

I wondered if he was going to pop round the house that evening. He didn't. I stayed in though, in case he did. The most extreme case of this that I have witnessed personally was a parting comment made by a seller on eBay. I had just purchased an item from him and we were exchanging pleasantries and addresses. He lived in Thurso, about 650 miles away. His final email to me finished with CU L8TR. He didn't turn up either.

The demise of the pubs

I don't know where you live, but where I live there were pubs all over the place. At one time, there would be three to four pubs in an average Valley village and that's not including the workmen's club, the rugby club, the miners' institute, the off-licence etc.

Nowadays, pubs that are still open are a rare sight. Even those that are open seem to change hands on a regular basis. Every now and again signs appear outside closed pubs heralding: "Grand Re-opening. Under New Management. Free Music, Free Pool. Darts, Big Screen, Bar Meals, Sunday Lunches."

They also sell 'exotic' drinks and cocktails that come with umbrellas, bits of fruit and sparklers to try to attract the more up-market clientele.

I remember going into one of these 'in places' and asking the landlady for a Double Entendre and she gave me one.

So when the grand re-opening comes along, people flock there. Soon the 'new' pub is the place to be. You're standing shoulder to shoulder, four deep at the bar, and can't hear yourself think because the free live band is blasting out 70s glam rock covers at volume levels which would make your ears bleed. Marvellous!

Then, the brewery notices the profits shoot up – this pub has lost money steadily for years, and look at it now! Raking it in.

In their wisdom, they up the rent and prices to such an extent that the new managers and tenants can't make a living, so they pack it in and the pub shuts down awaiting the next wave of "new broom sweeps clean" tenants to come in and make a go of it, and then the cycle starts all over again.

The only pubs that remain open long-term are those that are owned by the people who run them – but even now these are faced with another barrier which is affecting them very badly. I am referring to the smoking ban. Gone are the days when you could stand by the bar and have a chat and a fag with your mate. You can still have a fag, but you have to go outside for it. It's not too bad if the pub has a nice beer garden with a shelter in case of rain, but if your pub, like most Valley village establishments, is situated on the main street or the middle of a terrace, the only place smokers can go is outside the front door.

This in turn attracts animosity from passers-by who commonly complain of the fact that they have to cut their way through the fag smoke with a machete, put up with drunken foul-mouthed louts blocking and littering the pavement, people leaving glasses on the walkway etc. – it's a recipe for disaster!

Also, with the relaxation of the licensing hours, it's quite feasible that people may be drinking in a pub at 4am. What do they do if they fancy a fag? Do they stand outside and risk confrontation with the police? Someone's bound to complain about crowds of people smoking and chatting in the street at that time in the morning!

So, the odds have been stacked against pub-goers for a number of years now. Another, more crucial, barrier to the landlords' well-being is the price of booze elsewhere. I was shocked recently when I noticed in a local shop 6 litres of Strongbow on sale for a fiver. That's less than you'd pay for two pints in a pub.

It appears that because there is so much scope for confrontation, law breaking, inconvenience, prices, etc., people have started to do their drinking in the house.

You cannot re-create an authentic pub atmosphere at home really – I don't know of anyone who has a dartboard, pool table or skittle alley in their front room, so how far do they go?

In recent years, the pub quiz has been a great favourite and these are quite easy to stage in the comfort of your own homes and this is becoming very popular.

I am aware of quiz evenings that take place regularly in homes and friends take it in turns to go round each others' houses to compete with each other fuelled with cheap booze, savoury nibbles from Lidl – and a fag whenever they feel like it.

A quick browse around the internet will provide you with access to hundreds of net-based quiz questions; you can buy quizzes from compilers and don't forget the old favourite Trivial Pursuit. There is no shortage of provision available for home quizzers, and some even compile their own questions. These then spill over into the workplace when people want to share the quiz they did last night with their colleagues during lunch breaks.

I have participated in quite a few of these, but what intrigues me the most is the part where they tell you about some of the wrong answers that were given.

Here is a selection of my favourites – correct answers follow in brackets:

Q. "Geoff Hurst scored a hat-trick in the 1966 World Cup Final. Who scored England's other goal? Martin Peters. Oh, I've just given you the answer!"
A. "Georgie Best?" (Martin Peters)

Q. "In motoring terms what does OHC stand for?"
A. (After a long pause) "Oil Handbrake Carefully?" (Overhead Camshaft)

Q. "What is the length of an Olympic-size swimming pool?"
A. "It's the longest of the two sides, the other is called the width." (50m)

Q. "Cross-country skiing and rifle shooting make up which sport?"
A. "Polo?" (Biathlon)

Q. "Which game can be 'lawn' or 'crown green'?"
A. "Royal Tennis?" (Bowls)

Q. "Which word beginning with C is the name given to the electronic line judge at Wimbledon?"
A. "Cyberman." (Cyclops)

Q. "What is written in big letters on the back of a cricket Test umpire's shirt?"
A. "I'm not sure what it means but is it LBW?" (Fly Emirates)

Q. "On which card in a pack of playing cards is usually to be found the maker's mark and the copyright mark?"

A. "Isn't it on the box they come in?" (The Ace of Spades)

Q. "Who are the engine suppliers for the Williams Formula 1 team?"
A. "Is this a trick question? It isn't Williams. Go on, I'll say Astra." (BMW)

Q. "An Eskimo roll would be seen in which sport?"
A. "Is it one of those eating record endurance things? Ice cream is it? – Oh no, that's Arctic Roll. I'll just say Eating Championships." (Kayaking)

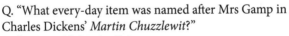

Q. "Which Paul was named Sports Personality of the Year in 1990?"
A. "I don't know any Pauls. I'll just say McCartney. I know it's not right." (Gascoigne)

Q. In chess, which piece must always stay on the same colour squares?
A. "The one that looks like a horse." (Bishop)

Q. "What every-day item was named after Mrs Gamp in Charles Dickens' *Martin Chuzzlewit*?"
A. "A Gamp?" (Umbrella)

Q. "In nature, the earth is composed of 3 main parts, the crust, the mantle and what?"
A. "The sky." (The core)

Q. "What is the name given to a succession of involuntary

spasms of the diaphragm causing a characteristic sound?"
A. "That's easy. A belch." (Hiccup)

Q. "What is the Aurora Borealis also known as?"
A. "Is it the technical name for eye sockets?" (Northern Lights)

Q. "A mixture of ground chalk and raw linseed oil is known better as what?"
A. "Semolina." (Putty)

Q."The density of which substance is measured by a lactometer?"
A. "Is it your boobs? You know when you have a mammogram." (Milk)

Q. "What did Adam not have that every other man does have?"

A. "Ribs." (Belly button)

Q. "What is the type of organism that lives on or in another called?"
A. "Siamese twins." (Parasite)

Q. "Which country voted to keep the Queen in 1999?"
A. "It wasn't us was it?" (Australia)

Q. "What's the second heaviest land animal?"
A. "A blue whale." (Rhino)

Q. "According to the proverb, when should you not count your chickens?"
A. "If they're all in the same basket." (Before they've hatched)

Q. "Who wrote the *Marriage of Figaro*?"

A. "Dickens?" (Mozart)

Q. "What was first crossed by tightrope by Charles Blondin in 1859?"
A. "The Atlantic Ocean." (Niagara Falls)

Q. "What's a young kangaroo called?"
A. "A skippy." (A joey)

Q. "What is a lexicon?"
A. "A sort of antelope?" (A dictionary)

Q. "Who went with Alice to Buckingham Palace?"
A. "The Queen of Hearts." (Christopher Robin)

Q. "In a 1967 Walt Disney film, by what other name was 'The man cub' known?"
A. "Baden-Powell." (Mowgli)

Q. "What is the English equivalent of nom de plume?"
A. "Something to do with feathers? Birds of a feather? Feather duster?" (Pen Name)

Q. "There are three types of adult honeybee, Queen and worker are two. What's the other?"
A. "Wasp?" (Drone)

Q. "What is acclaimed to be the most ferocious freshwater fish?"
A. "Crocodile." (Piranha)

Q. "What is a Codicil?"
A. "A young cod?" (An addition or alteration to a legal document)

Q. "Which is the only US state to start with the letter 'H'?"
A. "Ohio." (Hawaii)

Q. "Who succeeded Stalin as Communist Party leader?"
A. "Hitler." (Khrushchev)

Q. "What lies between Lake Erie and Lake Ontario?"
A. "The Lake District." (Niagara Falls)

Q. "What will be the next year that reads the same upside down and back to front as it does the right way up?"
A. "1111." (6009)

Q. "Which secret organization was founded in Pulaski, Tennessee in 1865?"
A. "The FBI." (Ku Klux Klan)

Q. "What is the other name for the Jewish day of Atonement?"
A. "Circumcision." (Yom Kippur)

3. Overheard in Wales

Spinnunputtunwerreezcassentbackenassent

I live in a very handy place with regard to access to large towns and cities. By car I can be in Newport in 15 minutes, Cardiff in 25 minutes, Bristol in 40 minutes, Gloucester in an hour, Swansea in an hour and a half, etc.

I've noticed that the West Country (which I have to travel east to get to, by the way) has quite a few little sayings and ways of expressing themselves that has baffled even me – the connoisseur of localisms!

The first time I had to ask for a translation was at the old Eastville stadium, once the home of Bristol Rovers, now the home of Ikea. I resided in Bristol for a while and used to watch both Bristol clubs, City or Rovers – whoever was at home. I didn't have any particular affinity to either team. I just liked watching football.

I was watching Bristol Rovers play Plymouth Argyle, must've been about 1980. There was a lot of crowd trouble at this game and during the match there was a substantial 'scuffle' behind one of the goals. This area was occupied mainly by Argyle supporters and it seems that a large Bristol fan had managed to get himself into this end and started the trouble.

When the trouble had 'boiled over' this large Bristol fan leapt the fence and ran diagonally across the pitch from behind the goal and was heading for my enclosure, pursued by police and stewards. Fair play to the guy, he beat his pursuers across the pitch and there was nowhere else for him to go – apart from into the crowd in the enclosure. He leapt the fence and, as I watched his progress, I realised that he was surely going to land on me! I instinctively put my hands out to protect myself and, as he descended, my hands made contact with his shoulders and I gave him a little mid-air shove which effectively broke his fall. He obviously misread the situation and assumed that I had purposely broken his fall and he was very grateful.

The on-pitch pursuers gave up the chase at this point and the police and stewards who were in the enclosure started making their way through the crowd towards him. Even though he was still a six-foot-seven fugitive, he found the time to give me a big cwtch to acknowledge the fact that I'd helped him to the ground and said:

> "Ere, oi thought oi were big but there's a bloke over there and he's gert 'uge."

I must admit, I had to refer the term "gert 'uge" to some of the Bristolians who were near me at the time because I had never come across anything like that before. Apparently "gert 'uge" is a West Country term to describe something that is very large.

But let's not dwell on football hooliganism, it's time to move on to explain what must be the most unusual chapter subtitle that has appeared in any book written in the English language. I am talking, of course, about the word:

> "Spinnunputtunwerreezcassentbackenassent."

For ease of reading, and for those who would like to try to pronounce it, I have broken it down into what I believe are manageable chunks and the pauses are placed where I believe they should be in order to identify the syllables accurately. Here it is:

"Spin-nun-putt-un-wer-reez-cassent-back-en-assent."

The quotation comes from someone who would prefer to be anonymous but whose real name is Mark Richards, a Bristolian, who reported hearing this when at work. It came about when a work colleague noticed that another colleague had parked his car in such a way that he could not reverse it back out of his precarious parking spot.

He came bursting into the workshop and announced this to all the other people, in a derisory and patronising way to describe their unfortunate colleague's parking dilemma.

I think a rough translation would be:

"He's been and put it where he can't back it, hasn't he?"

What do you think?

Although this is most certainly a phrase, Mark assures me that, at the time of delivery, "Spinnunputt-unwerreezcassentbackenassent", was actually pronounced as one word, no pauses, no hyphens, one word! And everyone understood it!

Mark said that this was a classic example of 'Pure Bristolian,' but I have my hands full trying to get my head around our local foibles, so I'll leave it here.

It must be said however, as a word "Spinnunputtun-werreezcassentbackenassent" is gert 'uge.

It must also be said that it's nothing to compare with our very own *Llanfairpwllgwyngyllgogerychwyrndrobwllllantysil io-gogogoch,* is it?

In fact, in Bristolian, it's gert 'uger!

If you ask Google for the longest place name in the UK, it will steer you to a place called:

"Gorsaf-awddacha'i-draigodanheddog-leddollôn-penrhyn-areurdraethceredigion."

This means: "The Mawddach station and its dragon teeth at the northern headland road on the golden beach of Cardigan Bay."

Sadly this was contrived by the railway to be used for publicity and to outdo *Llanfairpwllgwyngyllgogerychwyrndrobwllllantysiliogogogoch*, so because it is obviously a fake I will not mention it here.

This means that *Llanfairpwllgwyngyllgogerychwyrndrolllantysiliogogogoch* is officially the gert 'ugest place name in the UK.

Stereotypical nicknames for the Welsh

These fall into two categories:

1. Nicknames for us
2. Our nicknames for ourselves

In the first case, for the people who reside in the rest of the UK, Taffy or Taff is a pretty standard nickname for us of Welsh personage. Of course there are also the various derogatory sheep-based references to the fictitious belief that we have a penchant for indulging in activities that would be regarded in most circles as unnatural.

Unfortunately, that seems to be that. Having travelled a fair bit I have not come across any other nicknames when people have been referring to me or any other Welsh people for that matter – unless these have been made behind my back for fear of experiencing first-hand such cutting remarks as: "Yeah, we sh*g em, you eat em."

I've heard that one quite a few times and that's a bit of a show-stopper, inasmuch as I have never heard an adequate comeback to it. What can you say, to be fair, to a remark like that?

The first nickname I remember being daubed with came about in the early 1960s as a result of the seemingly constant need for the local authority to vaccinate all infant and junior school pupils against all sorts of strange diseases – TB, Smallpox, Typhoid Fever, Hepatitis C, etc.

One of my peers suddenly blurted out, whilst pointing at me 'Daifoid Fever!' when we were being consulted on the next bout of injections that we were going to be subjected to. This caused a great deal of hilarity amongst the rest of the class and a great deal of pain for the perpetrator after he had been yanked out of the multitude and thrashed by the teacher who was speaking to us at the time – yes, you could do that in those days! Needless to say, the nickname stuck and this was the one that stayed with me until I went to college. Nobody knew me there so Daifoid Fever became obsolete – soon to be replaced with a new one 'Olga.'

My peers decided to call me that following gymnastics lessons and was a reference to the very high-profile Russian gymnast Olga Korbut, who, in 1972 and 1976, dominated the Olympic gymnastics competitions. Unfortunately, the nickname did not reflect my prowess in the gym; it was a sarcastic snipe at my complete lack of flexibility, co-ordination and spatial awareness. I became world famous in college for being the worst gymnast that had ever darkened its doors and, needless to say, until the time I left in 1978, I was affectionately known as Olga. Thanks guys.

Just after college, I became a guitarist and synthesiser operator for a Cardiff band and I was immediately re-christened with the moniker 'Dai Synth.' In some circles, I am still known by that name and even now I sign certain

Christmas cards as 'Dai Synth' because if I used my surname I guess the recipients wouldn't know who the card was from.

More recently I found out that my students were calling me 'Dai Skusstin'. This came about after I had interrupted a conversation that I overheard and commented to the group, "It's got to be said, guys, that your language is absolutely disgusting!"

One lad, at the time, shouted, "Whahey! Dai Skusstin!" which caused a brief ripple of laughter amongst the group – I even appreciated that one – but I didn't realise that the name was in common use. Until a student that I didn't know approached me in the corridor and said "Er… excuse me, are you Mister Skusstin?"

I assured him I wasn't. He looked a bit embarrassed and went on to say, "The thing is, I'm new and I'll be joining your group next week and the other lads said that you was the bloke I had to see."

It was then that I spotted a few lads about 15 yards away, attempting to stifle their giggles and trying to look nonchalant, and I realised that one of them had told the fresher that he had to speak to Dai Skusstin, "There he is by there, go and see him now."

This brings me into the second case of nickname protocol – the statutory 'Dai' introduction. It's quite easy to see why I had been given the names, Daifoid Fever, Dai Synth and Dai Skusstin – my name is Dai, so it makes sense.

What may not make sense, however, is the way that we construct nicknames with the statutory Dai opening and the tagline will have something to do with the person's occupation, interest or idiosyncrasy – usually derogatory or patronising – in this case, having the Christian name David or Dai is not a prerequisite.

Here are some examples:

I remember a local traffic warden who was a particularly

unpopular chap and was known by everyone on his patch as 'Dai Book-and-Pencil.'

Another 'Dai' was 'Dai Pigs.' He was a local farmer, albeit a sheep farmer, but he was 'Dai Pigs' as far as everyone else was concerned!

Then there was 'Dai Wheel' – the garage owner – and 'Dai Beard' – a physics teacher who sported a beard. You're getting the hang of it now.

Before you get too cocky, see if you can enlarge on these two. Both seem to me to be a bit contrived but I'm assured that at some time these people existed and responded to the names they were given. The first is:

'Dai Central-Eating.'

I would not criticise anyone who assumed that Dai Central-Eating is a plumber. Well, it makes sense; unfortunately, the poor soul in question only had four teeth, two top front teeth and two bottom front teeth, hence the Central-Eating tagline. Aw bless.

The second is:

'Dai Eighteen-Months.'

I'd agree that this is a bit obscure and I could understand if no-one came up with an interpretation for that one. The story goes, Dai Eighteen-Months had lost half of an ear in an accident, and now he only had an ear and a half! (Please take into account our tendency to pronounce the word ear as year.) Oh please!

I was also told of a 5-a-side works football team who played other work-based teams on Wednesday nights. They called themselves 'Dai Five'. The members were: Dai Gin, Dai Gogg, Dai Dwp, Dai Dog and Dai Strap. Interestingly,

no team members were called 'David' and the goalie was female!

Top UK progressive rock band based in Cardiff, The Reasoning, have also adopted the 'Dai' persona. Like 'Dai Five', their band names follow a pattern that is now becoming familiar to us all.

Line up:

> Matthew, aka 'Dai Towels', because he always had towels on stage with him.
> Rachel, aka 'Dai Knick-Knacks' – apparently you could see her knickers through her skirt!
> Vinden, aka 'Dai Pigeons', because he did a superb pigeon impression.
> Band photographer, aka 'Dai Clicks', presumably because of the noise his camera made.

According to Matthew, someone loosely connected to

the band was such a great fan of the band names that he requested a name of his own. The band came up with the moniker 'Dai FOS' and he was chuffed to beans with this, even when told that FOS was an acronym for 'Full of Sh*t!'

On a slightly different tack, I have also spotted another Dai-related twist.

David Davies is a fairly common name in these parts and I can say that I actually know three people who bear this name and are affectionately known as 'Dai Twice'.

I don't know if that is commonplace in Wales but it is certainly something that crops up in the eastern valleys a lot.

I'll finish this section with a joke that actually appeared in *Welsh Valleys Humour*. Although it is an old joke, it perfectly illustrates this section:

> One morning, as Evan was on his way to the paper shop, he was approached by a stranger. A shady-looking fellow. The stranger spoke to Evan in a strong Eastern European accent. He said, "I am lookink for Dai." Evan thought for a moment and replied, "Dai the milk?" The stranger said, "No, no, it is Dai that I am lookink for." Evan replied, "Dai the bread?" The stranger sighed and said, "No, please listen to me, I vont to speak to Dai." Evan replied, "Dai the coal?" The stranger whispered into Evan's ear, "The sun shines brightly over the meadow in summertime." To which Evan retorted, "Oh, you mean Dai the spy, he'll be down the club by now."

I'm not sure you meant to say that

Sometimes people say things that don't come out quite right. Sometimes they mean to say something and say something else. Sometimes they say things that just don't make sense at all. This section looks at examples of things that weren't meant, but still said, nonetheless.

Here is a story of someone who did just that.

A guy walked into a pub and asked for "A bint of pitter and a larf of hager please."

"You meant a pint of bitter and a half of lager didn't you?" said the barman.

"That's what I said!" retorted the customer.

"No," said the landlord, "what you asked for was a bint of pitter and a larf of hager."

"I beg your pardon," said the customer sheepishly, "yes, I do want a pint of bitter and a half of lager. I'm doing that a lot lately."

"What?" asked the barman.

"Getting my words mixed up. I did a classic this morning," the customer added.

"Go on," said the landlord.

"Well I got up this morning, came downstairs and my missus asked me what I wanted for breakfast. Well, all I had to say was 'bacon and eggs' and you'll never guess what I came out with."

"Tell me," said the expectant barman.

"Well," the customer went on, "I came out with: 'You've ruined my life, I wish we'd never met, you horrible cow!'"

Another tale tells of a customer going into a butchers shop and asking for "A pound of kiddlies please." The butcher looked up and replied: "Don't you mean kidneys?"

"That's what I said, diddle I?" retorted the customer indignantly.

Now for a real story.

I was standing in the lottery queue at Morrisons one Saturday lunchtime when I espied a woman, laden with carrier bags, obviously flustered and in a rush heading for the door. Just as she got by me, she blurted out, to no-one in particular "Oh, I suppose I'd better do the lottery."

She joined the queue behind me, dumped her bags and began hunting through her handbag for her purse. When she located it, she put her baggage down at her side, and said to me: "Knowing my luck, the week I don't do the lottery will be the very week I win it!"

TO MAKE THINGS EVEN WORSE, DAI WAS STARVING

To be honest that's not the way it works. The week you don't do the lottery will never be the very week you win it. Quite the opposite, in fact.

I know what you're thinking: she has her regular numbers and she was concerned that they might come up if she didn't put them on. I thought that's what she meant as well – makes sense doesn't it.

When I'd paid for my lottery, I moved to one side to put the tickets in my wallet and I heard her ask for a Lucky Dip. Hmm. That'll teach me to make assumptions.

Here are quite a few more real ones, all heard in public – shops, pubs, bus stations, etc: anywhere, in fact, where the public gather to provide me with new material.

"I'm going to prove him wrong with a capital R."

"Things go in his ear and stay there. Then, he walks out the door and leaves me holding the biscuit."

"As usual, there was a lot of deep and deviousness about it."

"I'll give you a definite yay, hey or nay in half-an-hour."

"You gotta be able to read your own mind if you work here."

"I thought I'd ask you or you'd think I was gun-jumping in front of the pack."

"See, I didn't jump the pack in front of the gun did I?"

"I'll be back to you now in two shakes of a lamb's jiffy."

"Time is the essessence of the whole thing."

"We have it 999 per cent of the time and don't be so pedistic about it." (Pedantic)

"All you see me as is a clean cook and washle-botter."

"The bus is either on time or it comes either side. It's either on time or if it's not it's early or late."

"I don't mind eating chicken as long as it's not on the bone. It makes me feel like a cannibal."

"He may have fleas, he keeps on pruning himself." (Preening)

"You lot are like lemons jumping off a cliff." (Lemmings)

"I filled in the forms for industrial deafness five weeks ago and I haven't heard a thing since."

"Turn some of these lights off, it's like the blackberry eliminations in here." (Blackpool Illuminations)

"Don't tell me he's busy – just sat there doogling over that pad all day."

"I didn't plan it, it was all on the spur of the cuff."

"I think he's brain-dead from the ankles down."

"Er… do you parlez any Anglais at all?"

"Cast your mind back for a minute to next Tuesday."

"Indescribable is the only way I can describe it."

"Actually, going abroad for your holidays can work out cheaper than going abroad in this country."

"This war started long before we struck the first blow."

"They don't often break down, but when they do they don't work."

"Whoever wrote that sign must have been dyslexive."

"That new haircut of yours has gone to your head."

"In the 60s, you could go out dancing every night of the week – and Sundays!"

"And we didn't stop from the time we started 'til the time we stopped."

"Some steel fell off the lorry and decaffeinated him."

"I had a Waldorf salad." The reply. "What's Waldorf's?"

"Calm down please. The gymnasium is not the place to run around in!"

"Why do nudists go around dressed like that."

"Don't worry if I'm out when you ring me because my answering machine will be in anyway."

"Nowadays there's so much fighting and violence about. It was never like this in the war."

"I like that film *Battle of the Rose* with Danny DeFrutti." (DeVito)

"Sorry about all the trouble and apologise to the high Iraqi in your company for me." (Hierarchy)

"If you'd killed me every time you said you were going to I'd be dead by now."

"The mother is alright but the baby's in an incinerator... no not incinerator, one of those cucumber things." (Incubator)

"I've got work coming at me from more angles than even Hypotenuse could think of."

"That's six of one and 50 per cent of the other."

"If I gave up smoking for six weeks I'd save enough money to be able to afford to buy about 1,000 Benson & Hedges."

"We're in the middle of the deep blue sea."

"And that's not all, that's just the iceberg of it!"

"He had them running round in blue circles like headless flies."

"Who wants leg and who wants breast – there's only two legs, mind."

"Shut your mouth and eat your food."

"It was so cold you could cut yourself with a knife."

"And you can bet your bottom topper they won't do it."

"They reckon the first three minutes of life can be dangerous –
the last three can be pretty dodgy, too."

"He won't forget, he's got a head like an elephant."

"Alan has picked up a bug."
"What! And he ate it?"

"If we're lucky we'll be able to get everything we want in
here apart from the things we're going to have to get from
somewhere else."

"We're a sort of semi-professional, half semi-amateur set-up at
the moment."

"At the moment I'm not in a posituation to comment on it."

"Come on now, a bit of pain won't hurt you."

"What does RSVP mean?"
"I think it means 'Reply As Soon As Very Possible'. "

"The only English thing on the menu was a Spanish omelette."

"He came in with a face like a long violin."

"I always dry my hair with my head upside-down."

"It's on the floor by your left-hand foot."

"I don't like being shut in. I'm crosstopholdic."
"You mean chlorophoric."

"It's much better than feeling depressed and committing suicide
and I've done that before now."

"Is Easter Tuesday after Easter Monday?"

"Are there any cold drinks in the vending machine?"
"Only hot chocolate."

"Behind Closed Doors is about to start. Sorry I mean Whose House Is It?" *(Through the Keyhole)*

"I'm as cool as custard."

"Every time I open my mouth some stupid idiot speaks!" (A teacher scolding his class)

"How can he be Foreign Secretary if he isn't foreign?"

"He reckons he's a bit sidekick." (Psychic)

"You must think I was born under a banana boat."

"I wouldn't say I was superstitious, maybe just a tiny bit stitious."

"Do you have Bonfire Night in Germany?"

"Are the Chesterfields still going?" (Chippendales – male erotic dance troupe)

"That Chinese guy is totally work oriented."

4. Valleys Jokes

Stories depicting Valleys life

Dai goes on *Dragons' Den* and shows them a shotgun and an empty sack. Peter Jones says "So what's your business idea?" Dai replies, "Its a very simple concept Peter, just put the money in the bag!"

* * *

Evan was reminiscing with Will, "I'll never forget how happy I was when I saw my missus walking down the aisle towards me. My heart was beating fast and the excitement was unbearable. It seemed to take an age, but eventually there she was, standing beside me… I gave her a loving smile and said, 'Get that trolley over here love. They're doing three packs of Hobgoblin, for the price of two.'"

* * *

Gwen and Idris, an elderly couple are taking a stroll through the glorious Welsh countryside when they espy a fence where they used to conduct their courting. Excited by this, they make love furiously, with their arms and legs waving about everywhere. When they are finished, Gwen says, "You never had sex with me like that fifty years ago." To which Idris replies, "That wasn't an electrified fence fifty years ago."

* * *

Sian texts Sion on a cold winter's morning:
   "Windows frozen."
   Sion texts back:
   "Pour some luke warm water over it."

Sian texts back:

"Computer completely buggered now."

* * *

Idwal was bored and for some reason decided to paint the toilet seat. When his wife Rhian came home, he forgot to mention it. She went to the toilet and the paint was not quite dry – as a result she got 'stuck to the seat.' Idwal draped a large towel over Rhian's predicament and drove to the local GP's surgery. When it was their turn, Idwal whipped the towel off and said, "Doctor, have you ever seen anything like this before?"

"Well, yes of course," the doctor replied, "but never framed."

* * *

You admit to having broken into the dress shop four times?" asked the judge.

"Yes," said Gwilym.

"And what did you steal?"

"A dress, Your Honour," Gwilym replied.

"One dress?" echoed the judge. "But you admit breaking in four times!"

"Yes, Your Honour, the first three times my wife didn't like the colour."

* * *

A lot of people try to do the Welsh accent. A friend of mine said, "I can never do the Welsh accent. If I try it comes out Pakistani."

I said, "Well Ahmed, you're going to have to try a bit harder aren't you."

* * *

Dai was sightseeing on top of a cliff with his friend Dic. Suddenly, Dai said, "I think I'll have to go home, I've come over all giddy and I feel sick."

Dic said, "Have you got vertigo?"

Dai replied, "No I only live down the road."

* * *

Three Englishman walk into a bar and spot a Welshman sitting alone at a table. One fellow said to the others, "Let's pick a fight with that Welshman over there." His partner replied, "Wait, we don't want to be arrested. Let's make him start the fight." The third Englishman said, "Wait here chaps. I know how to do it." He went over to the Welshman and said, "St David was a sissy."

To this the Welshman replied, "Ah well you don't say!" and calmly resumed drinking his beer. The second Englishman now tried his luck and said to the Welshman, "St David wore a dress!" The Welshman again replied, "You're very sharp, you don't say!" and calmly resumed drinking his beer. The last Englishman told his friends he knew how to rile the Welshman and bounced up to the table and yelled, "St David was an Englishman!"

And the Welshman says, "Yes. That's what your mates have been trying to tell me."

* * *

An elderly man lay dying in his bed. While suffering the agonies of impending death, he suddenly smelled the aroma of his favourite Welsh cakes wafting up the stairs.

He gathered his remaining strength, and lifted himself from the bed. Leaning on the wall, he slowly made his way out of the bedroom, and with even greater effort, gripping the railing with both hands, he crawled downstairs. With laboured breath, he leaned against the door frame, gazing into the kitchen.

Were it not for impending death's agony, he would have thought himself already in heaven, for there, spread out upon waxed paper on the kitchen table were literally hundreds of his favourite Welsh cakes.

Was it heaven? Or was it one final act of love from his devoted Welsh wife of sixty years, seeing to it that he left this world a happy man?

Mustering one great final effort, he threw himself towards the table, landing on his knees in a rumpled posture. His aged and withered hand trembled towards a cookie at the edge of the table, when it was suddenly smacked by his wife with a spatula.

"Sod off," she said, "they're for the funeral."

* * *

Rhys went to the opera in Cardiff and was so disgusted that the soprano couldn't hit the E flat above high C, he left the auditorium and went into the bar for a drink. When the barman told him the price of his order, he hit the note himself!

* * *

Dewi was walking home worse for drink and was stopped by the police around 1am. The copper asked him where he was going at that time of night.

Dewi said, "I am going to a lecture about alcohol abuse and the effects it has on the human body."

The officer scoffed, "Really? Who is giving that lecture at this time of night?"

"Angharad," slurred Dewi.

The copper enquired further, "And who would Angharad be?"

"My missus," came the reply.

* * *

A farmer in Wales sees a bloke drinking from his stream and shouts, "Oi, you don't want to be drinking that, it's full of horse piss and cow shit."

The bloke says, "I'm from London and I've just purchased

a property in the village. Can you speak bit slower please. I can't understand your accent."

The farmer replies "If – you – use – two – hands – you – won't – spill – any."

* * *

A Welshman and an Englishman go to a pastry shop.
The Englishman whips three biscuits into his pocket with lightning speed. The baker doesn't notice. The Englishman says to the Welshman: "You see how clever we are? You'll never beat that!"

The Welshman says to the Englishman: "Watch and learn, a Welshman is always cleverer than an Englishman."

He says to the baker, "Give me a biscuit, I can show you a magic trick."

The baker gives him the biscuit which the Welshman promptly eats. Then he says to the baker, "Give me another biscuit for my magic trick."

The baker is getting suspicious but he gives it to him. He eats this one too.

Then he says again: "Give me one more biscuit..."

The baker is getting angry now but gives him one anyway. The Welshman eats this one, too.

Now the baker is really hacked off, and he yells: "And where is your famous magic trick?"

The Welshman says: "Look in the Englishman's pocket."

* * *

Bethan: "I need a new dress."

Dai: "What's wrong with the dress you've got?"

Bethan: "It's too long and the veil keeps getting in my eyes."

* * *

"Hello, is this Swansea Police?"

"Yes. What do you want?"

"I'm calling to report about my neighbour John Jones. He is hiding marijuana inside his firewood."

"Thank you very much for the call, sir."

The next day, the Police descend on John's house. They search the shed where the firewood is kept. Using axes, they break open every piece of wood, but find no marijuana. They apologise to John and leave.

An hour later, the phone rings at John's house: "Hey, John. Did the Police come?"

"Yeah!"

"Did they chop your firewood?"

"Yep. Cheers butty."

* * *

Huw called the RSPCA and said, "I've just found a suitcase in Ffos Las woods containing a fox and four cubs."

"That's terrible," the inspector replied. "Are they moving?"

"I'm not sure, to be honest," Huw said. "But that would explain the suitcase."

* * *

Dafydd was caught poaching in the river belonging to the local Squire, and was questioned by the local bobby. "Didn't you see the sign on the river bank?" he said. Dafydd replied, "Yes, it said 'Private' in big letters on the top, so I didn't read the rest of it."

* * *

A guide at Cardiff museum told a school party that the dinosaur that was facing them was 120 million and thirteen and a half years old. The pupils' teacher asked him how he could be so specific. He said, "When I started here I was told it was 120 million years old and I've been here for thirteen and a half years."

5. Final thoughts

Football

Wales is usually associated with rugby – often when Welsh people are abroad, in the UK and elsewhere. Non-Welsh people seem to think that a conversation on rugby is an appropriate way of starting off a conversation. It is fair to say that rugby is very high profile, especially during World Cups and Six Nations tournaments. On the whole I believe that interest in the game at grass roots level is fairly localised to the southern part of the country – there is certainly not the same level of interest in the game in mid and north Wales. Is it our national sport? Maybe. If you use participation as the quantifying factor, I would guess that either darts or Bingo may head that list if you did a nationwide survey – with perhaps home quizzing slowly claiming third place!

But what of the dreaded round ball game? Sometimes it is taboo to mention football in mixed company. "Poof's game!" is, I think, the most common retort to someone who dares refer to football in public.

I have always borne the brunt of many such rebuffs because I have always preferred football to rugby and have never had any qualms about saying it. It seems that I am not alone. There is massive interest in the game and a common practice with Welsh football fans is that they have two favourite teams. One will be their local side and the other will be one of the glamour sides.

I know someone who supports Cardiff City and

Liverpool. I know someone else who supports Cardiff City and Man Utd. We all know someone else who supports Swansea City and Arsenal – and the list go on.

I was always interested to know why someone could support two sides and be equally passionate about both. I understand the local team interest – the chances are they were taken to watch their local sides by their dads as kids, but where did the affinity for the glamour side come from? I did a bit of research and discovered that the glamour side was usually the first love, with the affinity to the local side coming later.

One person who shed the most light on this anomaly is a staunch Sunderland supporter. People normally go for Liverpool, Man Utd, Arsenal, Chelsea or Spurs, etc., of the glamour sides to support. I have also noticed a big following for Aston Villa and West Ham in the locality. I was speaking to a shop owner in Abergavenny who told me that by far, the most popular side in that town was QPR. Strange.

Anyway back to the Sunderland supporter. He has two sporting loves. He is captain, scrum-half and coach of a local rugby side, and a Sunderland supporter.

I asked him "Why Sunderland?" His answer made a lot of sense: "Because they won the FA Cup when I first got into football."

Sunderland won the FA Cup in 1973. So for the last 39 years, up to 2012, he had supported Sunderland ever since on the strength of that one game. When you look at the standard glamour sides – your Liverpools, your Man Uniteds et al, you can see why they are still very popular because historically, between them, they have won just about all the domestic and a large number of European competitions over the last four or five decades.

So it seems that the glamour side becomes your first love

even before you are old enough for your dad to take you to watch your local team. Interesting.

I often wondered what would happen if your glamour side actually played your other team. Who would you want to win?

Over the years, local sides tend to be in different leagues to the glamour sides but occasionally these would be drawn together in cup competitions. What then?

I put the question to the Cardiff City and Liverpool fan I spoke of earlier. Because of the touchy nature of supporting two teams, he wished to remain anonymous but I can reveal here that his name is Paul Weare. Paul has a season ticket at Cardiff City and goes to watch Liverpool when Cardiff haven't got a game.

In 2012, the line-up for the League Cup final at Wembley was Cardiff City v. Liverpool! I asked him who he would be supporting on the day and he was very hesitant with the answer:

> "It's a difficult one for me Dai, to be honest. I wish it was either one or other in the final, not both. It'll feel strange for me to be in a different end to the Liverpool fans, even though I'm used to being in with the Cardiff fans. I guess I'll be pleased and sorry at the same time, whoever wins. I'll just go to the game and enjoy the day out I suppose. If you pressed me, I suppose I would have to say I'd want Cardiff to win."

As a young man, I played for Abercarn Rangers and we played teams from the Newport area and the eastern Valleys. I noticed in those days there was a tendency for teams to keep their village name and tag on exotic last names.

I mean Rangers is a fairly standard tag on to a village side. Other common ones are Rovers, United, Town, Athletic, etc.

When I say exotic, I mean names that are associated with foreign glamour sides. The first I noticed was a team called Inter Cardiff. This struck a chord with me because I instantly

C'MON THE ABER!!

QPR
Abergavenny Posse

ABERGAVENNY TOWN FC COULD ALWAYS RELY ON THEIR FANS TO SHOW THEIR SUPPORT IF NOT THEIR COLOURS!

thought of the two sides in Milan: Inter Milan and AC Milan. I wondered if there was an AC Cardiff who were Inter Cardiff's rivals.

Then I came across Caerphilly White Sox. Pinched from Chicago White Sox maybe? These teams were around when I was playing. I don't know if they are still in existence, but a quick scan of local sports pages tells me that the trend is still alive with teams names such as: Prendergast Villa, Cwmbrân Celtic, Pentwyn Dynamos, Avenue Hotspurs, Abergavenny Thursdays (is this to outdo Sheffield Wednesday?) and my favourite, Bettws Sociedad.

Keep the trend going I say. Let's re-christen all our local sides so that a league table would look just like a Champions League who's who. Here is the sort of table I'd like to see; it is fictitious and the table has been constructed to show the progress of my ideally-named sides midway through any fictitious season.

Pos.	Team	Pl	W	D	L	GF	GA	+/-	Pts
01	Dukla Cwmcarn	32	17	8	7	58	32	26	59
02	Ajax Ynysddu	30	17	6	7	47	31	16	57
03	Estudiantes de la Cwmfelinfach	31	16	6	9	39	27	12	54
04	Spartak Abertridwr	31	14	11	6	50	36	14	53
05	Mwnt Bromwich Albion	31	14	10	7	52	38	14	52
06	Pontlottyn Moenchengladbach	30	14	9	7	47	27	20	51
07	Fochriw Torpedo	30	15	5	10	31	25	6	50
08	Real Pontllanfraith	30	13	11	6	35	31	4	50
09	Pretending Pontllanfraith	31	14	7	10	36	33	3	49
10	Slightly Tongue-in-Cheek Pontllanfraith	32	14	5	13	44	37	7	47
11	Pontrhydfendigaid North End	31	13	6	12	49	46	3	45
12	Lokomotif Bedwellty	31	11	9	11	42	37	5	42
13	Deri Caledonian Thistle	31	12	6	13	33	41	-8	42
14	Argoed Hotspur	30	10	10	10	29	30	-1	40
15	Sporting Clube de Glangrwyne	31	10	10	11	36	43	-7	40
16	Abertwsswg Argyle	30	11	6	13	42	48	-6	39
17	Swffrydd Park Rangers	30	11	4	15	47	57	-10	37
18	Machynlleth of Midlothian	30	9	8	13	33	32	1	35
19	AC Abercarn	30	9	7	14	47	51	-4	34
20	Pontneddfechan de la Plata	31	7	10	14	30	41	-11	31
21	Glynceiriog St Germain	31	8	7	16	27	46	-19	31
22	Bayern Bargoed	31	6	7	18	28	44	-16	25
23	Hajduk Hafodyrynys	30	7	4	19	24	49	-25	25
24	Atlético Aberbargoed	29	6	6	17	24	48	-24	24

Come on, local team managers, at least consider my proposal. Notice how my local village's fictitious side is top of the table. I made it up so I can do that. Wouldn't you do the same?

The road-sign issue

Admittedly not unique to the Welsh Valleys, road signs have long been a bone of contention in Wales – particularly with habitual road users, lorry drivers from outside Wales, holiday-makers, sometimes even with the Welsh themselves. I don't know what it's like abroad. Are road signs in Canada in English and French? I don't know, I've never been there. In Belgium, a multilingual society where most people speak a plethora of languages, are road signs printed in French,

I THINK IT SAYS 'KEEP OUT'

CROESO
WELKOM,
DOBRODOSLI,
VELKOMMEN,
TERVETULOA,
WILLKOMMEN,
ALOHA,
BENVENUTO,
KARIBU,
VÄLKOMMEN,
CROESO,
NGIYAKWEMUKELA

WELCOME TO THE VALLEYS

Dutch, Flemish, Walloon, German? Not when I was there, road signs were either in French or Dutch, depending on where you were within Belgium. They weren't in both, that's the point.

Maybe signs should be in Welsh only, as most of the place names are, or come from, the Welsh language. That would be simpler than this crazy bilingualism that seems to me to be a political correctness thing.

If you go into any hotel these days you will see in large letters above the reception, the words Welcome, Welkom, Dobrodošli, Velkommen, Tervetuloa, Willkommen, Aloha, Benvenuto, Karibu, Välkommen, Croeso, Ngiyakwemukela and however many others they can fit in above the desk.

PROOF THAT BEING BILINGUAL CAN GIVE YOU A DIFFERENT PERSPECTIVE ...

If we are going to try to cater for everyone and make sure no-one feels left out (aw bless), then maybe we should insist that all road signs worldwide contain all known languages just in case an Ovimbundu tribesman gets lost in the Nagorno-Karabakh Republic and needs directions to the tennis club! This is a political issue, so I'm leaving it here.

Anyway, back to reality. Just because something is written on a professionally-produced sign and positioned at a roadside or on the side of a building, it doesn't mean that the information on it is correct. And, if your sign is bilingual, it doubles the scope for the information on it to be incorrect because there is a need for a translation.

In Cardiff, in 2006, there was a very misleading sign near a road junction. It read: "Look Right" in English and "Look Left" in Welsh.

The best example of a mistake on a bilingual sign is most surely this one. Apologies to those of you who already know about this, but I just can't leave it out.

A local authority produced a sign, in English which read:

"No entry for heavy goods vehicles. Residential site only."

In order to comply with the bilingual policy, the phrase was emailed to their translation service provider and pretty soon, a reply was sent containing this text, in Welsh:

"Nid wyf yn y swyddfa ar hyn o bryd. Anfonwch unrhyw waith i'w gyfieithu."

So, having an emailed response to the request, the local authority had the sign produced with the English and Welsh versions on it.

Problem.

There was no-one in the office when the request went

through for translation. The emailed message was an automatic message sent to people to let them know the request was not being dealt with.

As we all know, the phrase, "Nid wyf yn y swyddfa ar hyn o bryd. Anfonwch unrhyw waith i'w gyfieithu" means, "I am not in the office at the moment. Send any work to be translated."

And this is what the sign that was erected said.

Don't believe me?

So, one thing we have to thank bilingual signs for is that little gem. Keep 'em I say, you never know when we're going to get another. Keep your eyes peeled and learn Welsh so you can be the first to spot them.

And finally

We have come to the end of what has become yet another deeply academic study of semiotics and sociolinguistics of the people of the South Wales Valleys.

And what a journey it has been. Not only have we looked at the two unpronounceable words in the previous sentence, we have examined: topography, pwp, glottal stops, glottal starts, pronunciation lessons, gastronomy, offlese, yoof cultcha, questioning and answering techniques, nicknames, things that came out wrong, the demise of the pubs, daft answers to quiz questions, football, bilingual road signs and the superb *spinnunputtunwerreezcassentbackenassents*.

I didn't realise that we could cover such a diverse range of topics in such a short time. There's so much to learn and it is fascinating to delve into the nitty-gritty of the world around us. I didn't realise there was so much in it. In fact, I learned a lot of things that I didn't know myself before I made them up when writing this.

We even ventured across the bridge, you know, the one of the Severn variety, and we did a bit of poking around over there, too. We even saved ourselves the £6.40 toll!

It's been about a decade since *Welsh Valleys Humour* came out and maybe in another decade or so we may have another – I wonder how much they'll be charging us to come home when we venture across the bridge by then? Whatever it is it'll be too much. Take a tip from me, stay here. It's cheaper and it's nicer, and having read this, you will be able to understand what the locals are saying to you.

Tra (Welsh for ta-ra).

TRAAAAAA!

Now go back to...

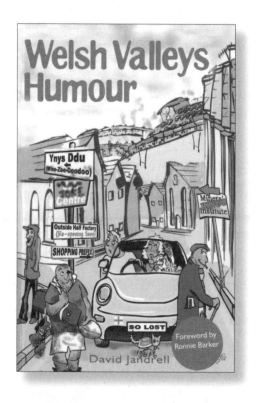

Don't miss out on the original volume of Valleys humour, lifestyle and argot – at still only £3.95!
For a full list of publications, go to our website,
www.ylolfa.com, where you may browse and order online – but support your local bookshop if you can!